Falling Into Ease
Simple Everyday Practices
to Release Struggle and Create Ease In Your Life

A Personal Guidebook

Scorpio Press
Published 2016

First Edition 2016

ISBN 978-0-9976105-2-9

www.Scorpio.Press

Index

Welcome!

I'm so glad you are here. This is the companion guidebook for *Falling Into Ease ~ Release Your Struggle And Create A Life You Love.* This book is designed to help you dive deeper and clear the way to living a life of ease. The following pages are a mix of journaling questions, meditation, writing exercises and other practices to generate the awareness process. Together they will support you as you eliminate suffering and step into not only a life of ease, but also begin to live your dreams!

Here is a bit of information that will help you make the most out of this Guidebook.

Journaling Questions

Journaling questions generally involve a stream of consciousness writing, writing without thinking, allowing the words to flow from your innermost being onto the page. They will typically have a number of questions for you to contemplate as a jump start. Try to bypass your mind and not think about those questions, but rather allow them to seep into your consciousness and let the writing flow. Sometimes you may wish to explore a stream of consciousness journaling with the non-dominant hand. This helps to bypass the thinking mind.

The writing exercises are more of a thought based process. Answer each of these questions in the order that they are presented.

This Guidebook is intended as a journal, meditation guide, releasing exercise and a whole lot more. In short, it is an organic, living thing and you should definitely WRITE, DOODLE & DRAW on these pages!

Journaling:

Getting Started

Why are you reading this book? What do you hope to gain? What are you looking for that you aren't experiencing?

Meditation:

Sit up comfortably in your chair and close your eyes. Take a few deep breaths in and out allowing your body to become still. Breathe in for the count of four, hold for a count of four and exhale for a count of eight. Do this five times. Bring your awareness deep into your body, moving from your mind to the tips of your toes and bottoms of your feet. Bring your awareness up your legs and into your hips. Breathe.

Bring your awareness to the palms of your hands, moving up your arms to your shoulders and neck. Nice and slow, breathing deeply all along the way. Bring your awareness to the back of your head and down your spine to your tail bone. Breathe. Bring your awareness to your belly, diaphragm and chest area.

Focus on your heart for four more breaths. Rest here for as long as you'd like. Take one more long deep breath in and exhale fully. Gently open your eyes.

Notice how you feel? What has changed? What else do you notice?

Get About the Business of Being Me!

*Get about the business of being you –
everyone else is already taken.*

Exercise:

Mirroring

Make a list of 10 people you highly admire.

Go back for each of the 10 people you wrote down, list three traits that you most admire about them. It could be things like: Trustworthy, Fun, Adventurous, Kind, Smart or anything that comes to you mind. Keep each item to a single word (or two if you have to), not a phrase or paragraph.

Take a look at the list of 30 traits that you wrote down. Identify those that are repeated by circling one and crossing out the others.

Write the circled traits from above in this list:

Take another look at your long list and move the most important or unique ones to complete a new list of seven.

This is who I've come here to be. Write the seven identified traits on these lines.

I am: _____, _____,

_____, _____,

_____, _____,

and _____.

If these resonate with you and you already own them, wonderful! If, on the other hand, you look at some of these and say, "Oh, this couldn't be me." I invite you to consider that these are in fact, who you have come here to be.

We cannot see or admire in another that which is not within us. If you don't recognize it yet, it might be time to take it on as an intention.

Take a few moments to write your response and reaction to this exercise.

Journaling:

Innermost Yearnings

Begin to contemplate what your heart yearns for. What are some childhood dreams that may have gone to the wayside? What do you love to do in your spare time? What did you love as a child? Write, stream of consciousness writing for at least 10 minutes.

Suffering is Not for the Weak of Heart

We do not have 100% control over the things that happen in our lives.

We do have 100% control over how we respond to it.

Exercise:

The Ways We Suffer

With the idea that we could end suffering, what would you no longer suffer with? (Of course, there are global issues, but let's keep this close to home.) Where in your life do you suffer?

What are the things and thoughts that cause you suffering? (Suffering in this exercise can be also things that irritate you, that you tolerate, that disgust you or cause you less than joy-filled thoughts.) List additional ways you suffer here.

Journaling:

Why Suffer?

What do you notice in doing the above exercise? What emotions are you feeling, what thoughts are going through your mind? What is in your subconscious about the reason for suffering, why do we suffer, as humanity? How do you feel about it? Write for a few minutes about what this exercise has stirred up for you.

Triple A's and Triple C's

Appreciation, Allowing, Accepting
Complaining, Criticizing, Condemning

The Golden Rule
What you do to others,
you do to yourself.

Journaling:

Appreciating, Allowing and Accepting

In what ways do you practice the Triple As of Appreciation, Allowing and Accepting? How do they show up in your life?

In what ways do the Triple C's, of criticizing, condemning and complaining show up?

Notice how you feel when you are operating in the A Zone compared to the C Zone. Notice what your mind does, how your body feels and what your emotional state is.

Meditation:

The Triple A's and the Triple C's

Sit up straight in your chair, with your feet flat on the ground. Close your eyes and begin deep breathing. Focus on your breath long enough for your body to relax and quiet. Bring your awareness to your feet and where they connect to the ground. (This helps get us out of our heads.) Notice how your body feels, how your energy is.

Notice how it feels when you are Appreciating life. Feel the feelings inside your body. Notice what you notice and keep breathing. Lean into the experience of Allowing. How does that feel in your body? What do you notice? Feel into Accepting. Is that different or similar to the others? Do you notice an expansion or ease or lightness?

Now bring to mind the C's – criticizing, condemning and complaining. Perhaps you can recall a moment of doing one of these recently. Without judgment, notice what happens to your body and energy levels when you activate the C's. Perhaps you find tightness in an area, perhaps your breathing changes, perhaps your energy drops. Simply notice what you notice while being aware of criticizing, condemning and complaining.

Come back to Appreciation. Do you notice an immediate shift in your body and energy? Activate Allowing and Accepting. Do you feel lighter again? Draw the experience of the A's into your being. Let the expansiveness permeate, penetrate and fill your being. Rest here for as long as you'd like. When you are ready, feel the openness all the way down to your feet once again. Anchor the experience. Gently open your eyes.

Take a few moments to write about your experience, any new awareness you might have or ideas that might have come to you.

In the Beginning

In the beginning when God created the heavens and the earth, God called it Good. In the beginning when God created humankind, God called it good! Love, Light, the earth, Us – it's all good!

Journaling:

Oneness – Impulse – Connection

If you knew that you were part of something that is so much greater than you, what would change? If you knew you were Creation expressing as the exact, perfect image of You, how might that affect you? If you knew that Creation is alive and well deep within your Being and you can recognize it as a quiet impulse in your core, what might it be saying to you? Allow these questions to spark a stream of consciousness, allowing your pen to write whatever comes.

Meditation:

In the Beginning

Sit comfortably in your chair with your feet on the ground and your palms open on your lap. Take a few deep breaths and allow your body to begin to relax; feel your mind quieting and your heart opening. As you quiet yourself, drop your aware-ness deep into your heart space, dropping from your physical heart, through the emotional heart and deeper yet into the Spiritual heart. Find your-self in the center of a beautiful field or meadow. What do you see? Look around and discover over on the edge of the field an escalator. It's a special one and you recognize it as such. Walk over to it and decide to take it down, down, down to the depths of creation and back to the beginning of time.

Step onto the escalator and begin your descent down. It is an adventure and feels exciting and very safe. As the escalator takes you down, begin to see your life, like a mural on the sides. See your current life, the last few decades; see yourself in your twenties and your teens. See your childhood. You see these times with no judgment, only cu-riosity and compassion. Simply notice what you notice. As the escalator continues its journey, see your infancy, and the time just prior to your birth in this life time. See the space between the worlds.

As your journey continues, the escalator takes you through the past millennium, to the first creation of humanity, then back further to the creation of multi-celled beings, to the first creation of life it-self. Drop deeper to time of the first light. In the beginning, when there was nothing as all, there came an impulse that was so great that it created out of nothing-ness, all things. In this impulse, You were first created and the impulse of creation continues in you today. The impulse is Love itself. Come to know Love, and you come to know your-self.

Discover what you discover at the beginning of time. Perhaps there is a guide there to greet you, to show you what you'd like to see or to answer questions. Perhaps you'd like to journey around for a bit. Take your time.

When you are ready, jump back onto the escalator and begin the journey forward in time, moving as quickly or slowly as you'd like, back to the present moment. Do not get off here, however, continue in time, into the future. Become aware of the impulse that is drawing you forward. What is it? What are the qualities and flavors of the impulse moving you forward? Feel and become the Love that is the impulse of Creation. What would Love do? What is

Love calling you to be and do? Explore here for as long as you'd like.

When you are ready, jump back on the escalator and return to present time, filled with a new appreciation and awareness of Love as Creation. As you return to your field, take a few deep breaths, anchor your experience and your new awareness into your being by placing your hands on your lower belly and saying, thank you!

Take a few moments to write about your experience in the impulse of creation and the beginning of time.

Useless and Unnecessary Suffering

*Life is filled with suffering and your work
is to separate the necessary from
the unnecessary suffering.*

Exercise:

Useless and Unnecessary Suffering

Here is a short list of the ways people suffer. Mark the ones you relate to.

Grief

Time lack

Lack of money

Not living the life of their dreams

Bosses – other people

Working for a living - rather than living for life

Self esteem

Worthiness

Guilt

The if only syndrome

Feeling separate

Alone and lonely

Dried up inside

Is this all there is???

What's the point?

Not believing

What is the one thing that keeps you from peace?

Add your own ways of suffering to the list.

Journaling:

Giving Suffering a Voice

What are your unconscious voices around suffering? Where do they show up in your life? Take a moment to list any others out. Let them have voice on paper. Don't worry you won't be taken over by suffering if you let it speak, in fact, it will lessen.

"Everything will be alright in the end. If it's not yet alright, no worries, it's not yet the end."
~Hotel Manager, The Best Exotic Marigold Hotel

Exercise:

Separating the Useless and the Unnecessary Suffering

Sit comfortably in your chair and begin to do some deep breathing. Imagine that all of life is found in an egg shell. It's your life and its full of all your experiences, circumstances and situations. Like a real egg, with the whites and the yolk; there are two parts in your egg. For simplicity and exercise sake, we will call them "Things that Happen" (yolk) and "Useless and Unnecessary Suffering" (white). With your eyes closed, imagine that you are cracking open this egg of yours and that you will be separating the yolk from the whites. Do you remember doing this as a child with your mama overlooking? First cracking the egg, then transferring it from one shell half to the other, allowing the whites to drop into the bowl and keeping the yolk whole and contained.

Do this for your life. Literally put your hands out in front of you and crack the egg, move your hands back and forth as you allow the parts to separate. When the whites have all dropped into your bowl and the yolk is the only thing left in the shells, you are complete. Put the yolk in another container.

Notice what you notice. Does your mind feel less cluttered? Is there a release in your emotions? How does your body feel?

Take a few moments to write about this exercise and your experience with it.

Meditation:

Breaking Open Your Heart

Close your eyes and take a few deep breaths. Feel your feet on the ground and your body in the chair, fully supported. Relax your body, quiet your mind and begin to bring your awareness into your heart. Imagine a great big, pink bubble of peace and love surrounding you. Relax into it. Wait until you feel your body relaxing, there will be a subtle shift.

Imagine taking your physical heart outside of your body for observation. Hold it in your hands as the sacred object it is. See it surrounded by a covering, like our egg shells in the previous exercise. Hold your heart, look at it, appreciate it. Speak with it, ask it if it has anything it would like you to know right now. Notice that the shell around your heart is wanting to break open, more like a bird hatching than an egg cracking. Can you let it crack open? Can you observe the love and peace that surrounds you supporting the breaking open of your heart?

Let it break open. And when it does, feel the love and peace filling it with the gentle pink energy. Feel the safety and freedom in allowing the outer container of your heart to break, freeing it to even more love and light; peace and joy. Imagine that this breaking open of your heart is symbolic for allowing more connection and more love into your life. Let your newly opened heart receive the love for as long as you'd like. When you are complete, become aware once more of your body, take a few deep breaths and gently open your eyes.

Take a few moments to write about your experience, any insights, awareness or messages you might have received.

Sublayers of the Heart

The desire to live in and from the spiritual heart is the impulse to awaken.

Journaling:

Listening to the Impulse of the Deeper Higher Heart

Begin to identify the layers of the heart, from the physical to the emotional and deeper yet to the spiritual heart. Listen deeply to the impulse of Spirit within you from the access point of the spiritual heart. Contemplate any particular times you've experienced bliss or the awakened state. Write freely and discover what the impulse has for you today.

Meditation:

Finding Love in the Deeper Heart

Close your eyes and take a deep breath in. As you exhale, relax. Focus for a few breaths on breathing deeply and fully exhaling. Become aware of your body. Feel your head and notice the backs of your eyes. Feel your feet firmly on the ground. Open your palms and become aware of them. Bring your awareness from the top of your head to your feet. Draw your awareness up through your legs, hips and torso, landing in your heart area. If you can't find your heart, drop again down into your hips and rest there for a moment.

Bringing your awareness up from your hips to your heart, feel it. Imagine seeing it, as the physical organ that is it, pumping blood, supporting life in your body. Imagine dropping into center of your heart, finding yourself in a cave of exquisite crystalline light. Feel the safety, the support, the security of being the safe place deep in your heart.

From the deeper heart, you can bask. You can rest. Here you are filled with light, love, energy and inspiration. Rest quietly here until you feel an impulse coming from the depths of your being. You are supported, you are loved.

Feel the love that is. The love that is for you, with you, as and in you. Feel the love that penetrates and permeates your being. Let this love overflow your heart and enfold your entire being. How much more love can you receive? Receive it and then a bit more.

When you are ready, feel this love moving throughout your body, into your feet, grounding it through your being. Feel it moving through your hands and head. Anchor the experience and bring it forward, back into this present moment. Gently open your eyes. And so it is.

Take a few moments to journal about your experience with this meditation.

Creating Space

The Truth About Surrender

*Surrender is simply a letting go or relaxation
resulting in the creation of space –
Space to Be, to breathe, to dream and create.*

Exercise:

Finding Hidden Patterns

Identify a habitual emotion, feeling or pattern.
Look for the emotional core of it, what gets triggered in you again and again? It could be fear, sadness, unworthiness, anger, resentment or anything else.

Allow one feeling to emerge. Activate it, let it begin to come alive in your system and awareness. Let the feeling build so you are feeling it in your body, not just thinking about it. This is very important. Find it, and bring it forward.

Begin to create space for the feeling. Typically, we want to push it down or away, this time, we are inviting it into our awareness, allowing it to simply be without any story about it.

Continue expanding the space around the feeling so it begins to flow. Follow the feeling through to its completion, creating even more space.

Exercise:

The Gift of Space

Give yourself a gift, create some space today! What are some physical ways that you can make space?

Take a bubble bath
Clear off a counter
Empty a drawer
Bring order to your wallet or purse
Straighten up a room
Sit for an allotted amount of time with a cup of tea
Have that conversation you have been avoiding

Create space to be. What will you do for yourself today to create space?

Meditation:

Surrender by Relaxing

Imagine that all your stress could be released as simply as exhaling. Sit down right now and do this. Take a deep breath in and hold it for a moment. Then let it go. Exhale, all the way, push the air out of your system and feel the space being made for new, fresh air. Inhale, hold and exhale, this time consciously letting the stress that might be in your body or mind release. Feel it falling off your body and going into the ground.

With each breath, let more stress release. Feel your shoulders dropping, your chest expanding, your neck and shoulders relaxing. What else do you notice? What happens to your jaw, your palms? Do your arms and legs get heavy? How is your brain? More open? A little less tied up?

Keep making more space by putting your aware-ness into for as long as you'd like. When you are complete, take another deep breath and exhale.

Gently open your eyes.

Take a few moments to write down any insights, experiences or awareness that you might have had.

Believe it Because We See it? Or See it Because We Believe it?

"Whatever the mind can conceive and believe, it can achieve."
~ Napoleon Hill, Think and Grow Rich.

Exercise:

What You Believe

Here are some beliefs some of us have that simply are NOT true. Put a check mark on the ones you identify with:

I'm unworthy
I'm not lovable
I'm wrong
I'm broken
The system sucks
Life is hard
If I work hard, I'll make it
My financial success defines me
I am my body
My family defines me
We are doomed on this planet

Add a few of your own beliefs here...

Here are few other beliefs – try them on for size. Do you believe them?

I am worthy
I am a success
I love, am loved, lovable
I can do anything I want
I love money and money loves me
I am One with All that Is and Infinite Possibilities
I am a child of God in whom God is well pleased
I have free choice to do with my life as I desire
I can have all that I want and more
I create my life
Life is good and meant to be fun and abundant and filled with joy

Add a few more here...

Which beliefs are expansive? Which are contractive? If you really could choose your beliefs, which would you choose? Why don't you? Journal about the awareness that comes in doing this exercise.

Journaling:

Choose a New Belief

Choose one new belief that you would like to instill and activate and write it down. Write about how you might be different with this new belief. Do a compare and contrast between the new belief and the old one. Take it on as a mantra for a week and see what happens. Say it out loud, repeat it to yourself, keep it top of mind, work it through your body – in your feet and hands, hips and belly, let it land in your heart. Can you begin to believe it as truth?

A Look at Fear

Resistance to what is, causes suffering.
Bring fear from the dark to the light
and it loses its power.

Exercise:

Our Fear

Take a look and feel into the following fears. Consider whether each one is a "real fear" or an "emotional fear."

- *Coming across an angry person in a store*
- *Facing a gun*
- *Sitting next to people who don't look like you*
- *Checking your bank account and finding out that there is no money left at the end of the month*
- *Standing on a cliff about to jump off on a zip line tether*
- *Taking off by yourself on a journey across the country*
- *Needing to tell someone you love something they don't want to hear*
- *Standing up to your boss*
- *Hearing strange noises outside your home in the dark*
- *The electricity going out and the storms coming*
- *The thought of losing everything material that you own*
- *Driving in a city you don't know*

- *Traveling abroad to country you are comfortable in*
- *Traveling to a country that scares you*
- *Watching scary movies*
- *Taking a leap of faith in a new career direction*
- *Sending your child off by themselves for the first time*
- *Watching your son race motorcycles, really fast*
- *Hearing or receiving a serious diagnosis for yourself or a loved one*
- *Watching a neighbor come to your door, who sucks your energy dry*
- *Hearing a particular voice in your head telling you to watch out*

What else activates fear in you?

What else brings you fear?

Identify those fears which are emotionally based and can be eliminated through conscious thought. What can you do to eliminate or reduce the amount of fear you experience?

Meditation:

Relax into fear

Feel the fear and do it anyway. Sit comfortably in your chair, close your eyes and open your palms. Breathe deeply for a few moments. Bring to your awareness these statements: "In the moment that we fully feel our fear, we are freed from it. We can then begin to embody a greater point of attraction." Let the statements bounce around in your awareness for a moment or two. Relax into any resistance that might be showing up. Relax again and begin to welcome the fear. Relax your body. Relax your mind.

Imagine you are letting go of the grip you have on fear, and it is being freed from you to go about its merry way. Let the grip that fear had on you loosen as well. Imagine that it slides right off of you, as you relax. Discover it was you holding it, not it holding you. Begin to cultivate a welcoming of fear. When you are able to be with it, you no longer have to resist it, buy in to it, try to change it or have it be different. Be with the fear you feel.

Notice that the fear no longer has any control over you. Fear may still show up, but now you have the capacity to breathe into it and take action anyway. Feel the spaciousness and the peace. Relax even more deeply now. Who would you be without fear?

Be that person. What would you do without the fear holding you back? Do that thing.

Explore this new way of being for as long as you'd like. Bring your awareness back to your heart and bask in the realization that you can welcome fear at any moment, and then you are freed from it. When you are ready, take one more deep breath and gently open your eyes.

Take a few moments to journal your experiences and insights from this meditation.

One Key To End Suffering for All Time

One key to end suffering for all time is to break the illusion of separation. ~Aliza Bloom Robinson

Meditation:

Breaking the Illusion of Separation

Sit in your favorite chair comfortably with your feet on the ground. Close your eyes and open your palms. Take a few deep breaths in and allow your body to relax, your mind to begin to quiet and your heart to open. Bring your awareness from your mind to your body, dropping it from your head to your chest; becoming aware of your hands and feet; arms and legs. Bring your awareness to your hips and rest there for a moment. Become aware of that part of you that is more than your body, it is your Essence.

Begin to drop your awareness with each exhale down through your body, out your feet and into the ground. With each breath, drop deeper, so that you end up at the core of the planet. Feel yourself grounded and connected, supported and nourished. Offer your gratitude to the planet and open to receive from her. You are one with Mother Earth, we all are One with Mother Earth and that makes us connected.

Bring your awareness slowly and gently back up through the layers of the earth and into your feet, drawing it up to the crown of your head. Send your awareness up through your crown out the roof of your building and up into the sky. With each exhale, now allow your awareness to be drawn up higher and higher until you reach the sun. Feel the expansion. Here you are lifted from daily life challenges into a field of Oneness.

Offer your gratitude and appreciation to the Sun, the Universe and Creation itself. Wait until you receive an energy returning to you. Here you are One with all that is and infinite possibilities. One with the stars and planets, one with the Universe and beyond.

When you are ready slowly and gently begin to bring your awareness back into your body, landing in your heart area. One with the earth, One with the Universe, One with all that is, you are whole, perfect and complete. Let this energy wash over you and fill you.

Knowing your Oneness breaks the illusion of separation. Bask here for as long as you'd like. When you are ready, slowly and gently bring your awareness back into the room you are in and say aloud: I am One with All that Is.

Repeat it as a new truth enters your consciousness and replaces the illusion of separation.

Spend a few minutes writing about your experience on Oneness and breaking the illusion of separation.

Exercise:

Choose Peace

Peace is a choice and a blink away. Where and how can you choose peace right now?

Bringing peace to every moment in your being, begins to bring peace to the world around you. Make it part of your daily practice to choose peace. To lay down that which is unlike peace, and choose again and again and again.

Remember a time when you were totally peace-filled. Write about it here.

Where does the world steal your peace?

What is the typical thing that causes you un-peace?

What can you do right now to begin to bring yourself back to peace?

If peace is a choice, how can you choose it? What
do you have to give up instead?

A Word About Emotions

Emotions are energy in motion (e-motion).

Exercise:

Discovering Emotions

List your most common emotions or emotional qualities.

How do you judge them? As good or bad?

Which ones would you like to keep? Circle them.

Which ones would you like to add? List a few you'd like to have:

Which ones do you wish weren't there? Where do you judge them? Can you let them be?

What did you discover?

Journaling:

Dialog with Emotion

Pick one of the emotions that you judge as bad or would like to eliminate. Imagine that is has a personality, a shape and color to it. Begin to dialog with the emotion. Write in a free flow manner allowing anything that comes up to be ok.

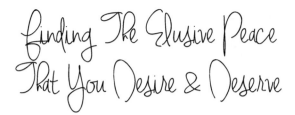

*Finding The Elusive Peace
That You Desire & Deserve*

EASE:
Effortless Awareness of Spirit and Excellence

Exercise:

*What Would Ease
Look Like in Your Life?*

What keeps you from living with ease? What are your reasons or excuses?

If you had ease, what would you be doing differently?

How can you bring more ease into your experience? What are some specific, concrete things you can do today?

Meditation:

Finding Light in the Dark

Sit comfortably in your chair with your feet flat on the ground and your palms open. Close your eyes and take a few deep long breaths in and out. Wiggle a bit to settle your body and open your heart. Find yourself standing in the center of a big, beautiful field. This field is your sacred place. Here you are safe and free, whole and peace-filled.

If you struggle with depression or procrastination or a heavy feeling hanging over you, imagine it now as a dark blanket covering you. (You can use any emotion or feeling here.) Can you imagine that this dark blanket is like the fort you used to build as a child in the safety of your front room? Even if you want to fight it to get it off, relax into it for a moment. Let the fort become safe and comfortable. Now let the dark blanket wrap you in its warmth. Remember snuggling deep into a comforter on a cold winter's night. Let it wrap you and relax into it even deeper.

Begin to peek out from under the corner of the blanket. Let a little light in and see that it is bright outside. Wiggle your foot so it also peeks out from the ends. Stretch your body like when you wake up from a long nap. The blanket is now just a blanket, slip out from underneath it and stand up tall. Free. Refreshed. Stretch into to your tallest and most empowered self. Take a look at the blanket laying there in a heap. Thank it for keeping you safe and warm, for being your companion for as long as it has been. Walk away.

Become aware of the sun on your face, the breeze on your arms. What shade of blue is the sky? Do you hear sounds of birds? Perhaps a running creek in the distance? What can you see that you haven't been able to see from under that blanket? Find a new possibility or pathway to follow. Perhaps there is something you are being called to do. Feel the new found freedom and lightness. Open your mind and heart to receive.

Bask here for as long as you'd like exploring the field of your Essence.

When you are ready come back to the center of the field, give thanks for the experience. Take a few deep breaths and when you are ready open your eyes.

Take a few moments to write about your experience in this meditation.

Would It Be Alright if Life Got Easier?

"Until one is committed, there is hesitancy, the chance to draw back, always ineffectiveness. Concerning all acts of initiative (and creation), there is one elementary truth that ignorance of which kills countless ideas and splendid plans: that the moment one definitely commits oneself, then Providence moves too. All sorts of things occur to help one that would never otherwise have occurred. A whole stream of events issues from the decision, raising in one's favor all manner of unforeseen incidents and meetings and material assistance, which no man could have dreamed would have come his way. Whatever you can do, or dream you can do, begin it. Boldness has genius, power, and magic in it. Begin it now."
~Goethe.

Journaling:

A Life of Ease

Imagine a life of ease. Write about it here in free flow stream of consciousness writing. You might use the previous exercise to get you started. What are you doing? How are you feeling? What are the conversations you are having with your friends?

Make it real and be sure to use present tense language.

Exercise:

What Would I Love?

What are your dreams?

Play with the question: What would I love?

Make the commitment to do one thing every day towards it.

The Great Grand Vision

"If one advances confidently in the direction of his dreams, and endeavors to live the life which he has imagined, he will meet with a success unexpected in common hours".
~ Henry David Thoreau

Exercise:

Stretching Our Dream Muscles

Let's play. Exercises to Stretch our dream and goal muscles.

If there were no limits in your life, what would you love, love, love to be doing?

If you had no worries about what others thought of you, what would you love?

If money were no issue...

If you had no voices in your head that said things like.... You can't, you shouldn't, you won't...

If you had only voices that said, "You go Girl! You go guy! You can do this... "

If time was no issue... what would you love? Where would you live? What would you do?

If you had no other obligations to care for others, family, kids, parents, spouses, etc... what then?

If you were writing the script of your life, in the dreamiest, grandest, movie, what would your life look like in 10 years? 20? 5?

If you were totally and completely fulfilled and content, what would you tell someone else who is stuck in "life as we know it?"

List out 20 reasons or excuses why you haven't achieved this yet. List them even if you don't want to acknowledge them or especially if you think you shouldn't be saying that.

Drop into your heart and feel into the dream again, as if it is already achieved. How would you feel?

What would you be doing differently than you are now?

What would you be saying?

Where would you be spending your time?

Who did you need to become, what did you need to embody in order to achieve this dream?

List two or three simple, concrete action steps that you can take today to bring aspects of you dream into manifestation right now. (Examples: buy some running shoes, get a travel brochure, make a vision board, etc.)

Journaling:

Embody the Dream

What do you have to embody in order to become who you need to be to be living this dream? Who do you need to become? If you were the person who already had this dream, what would you be doing?

Look deeper again, what is in the way of you embodying these things? Let's look at things like: unworthiness, unlovable, not enough-ness. What do you carry around like a badge that is simply not true, but we were taught it? Take a dive into the deeper stories that you tell yourself.

List them out on a separate piece of paper, write them all as they occur to you. List here things like anger or guilt. Find any reason still in your unconscious that you don't step into your dreams. When it feels complete rip up that paper! Be done with it!

Embody your dream and write it in the present tense using as many sensory words as possible. What are you doing, feeling, seeing, hearing, tasting, smelling, saying? How does it feel to be the person living their dreams?

Accessing the Subconscious

*The subconscious is like a huge mega-computer
and is quite easily programmable.
If you don't like the programs, change them!*

Exercise:

Exploring the Layers of Emotion

Take a breath and acknowledge what emotion you might be having right now. Allow the feelings you are experiencing to have free rein for a bit. Stop, take a look, feel them, name them and allow them. From allowing them, come to the place of accepting them. Oh, look at this I'm feeling hopeless right now. Become curious. Oh, that's curious. Wonder what that's about. Look gently with curiosity. Hmmm. Ok. What does hopeless (or whatever emotion you are working with) feel like?

Where in my body does it live?

Does it have a color or shape?

Can you draw it out in front of you into a container? What does that container look like?

Can you allow it? Can you accept it? Can you pick it up? Can you lift it to eye level? Up higher? Can you release it up into the universe?

If so, what do you find underneath it?

Is it another emotion? If so, look at it, feel it, name it and allow it.

Repeat the process of identifying and containing the next layer of emotion and see if you can lift it. Keep exploring the layers, if you have the time and space to do so until you find a spaciousness.
Write about this experience.

Meditation:

Quantum Leaping

Sit comfortably in your chair, close your eyes and take a few deep, long breaths. Find your heart space and relax for a few moments with your breath taking you deeper and deeper into yourself. Let's play with discouragement, (or use any emotion that is present for you). Activate it by remembering a time when you were discouraged. Look for it, feel it in your body and allow it. Accept that it is there. Here's a little trick here. We cannot make it go away, it is not about denying it or pushing it out of our systems. The magic comes in allowing it, accepting it and then transcending it.

Do not try to make emotions leave. They won't, they will only get stuck. Let discouragement come alive in you. You recognize it, it has a familiar feeling to it. Now step it up. As you allow discouragement, choose instead blame. NOTE: Why would you want to be in blame? Isn't that icky? Remember no, judgements on any emotions, they are simply energy trapped. Blame in and of itself does not feel good, you are right but from discouragement, because it is a step up, it feels better. Better is what we are going for. Then step up to worry. This is the stepping process. Often it takes time.

So now, let's go back to discouragement. Activate it again, allow it to be in your awareness. How does it feel? What does it look like? Because we can, let's activate the frequency of gratitude. Think of something that you are grateful for. It could be the sun, or breeze, or that fact that you are breathing. Simply activate gratitude. Find it, remember a time when you were truly grateful. Feel the activation in your body. What is happening? Stay with it for a few minutes. If you drop out of gratitude, activate it again. Use the energy and image of activation. Turning it on. Calling it in. Come into a vibration of gratitude and notice what you notice. Do you feel lighter? Are you in resistance to it? If so, take another few breaths. Perhaps you notice your breathing change? Perhaps your shoulders drop or tension is released. Let gratitude wash over your entire being. Bask in it.

When you are ready, anchor the experience of gratitude through your body, mind and emotions. Memorize the feeling. Take a few more deep breaths and gently open your eyes.

Take a few moments to write about your experience with this meditation.

In the Midst of Life

Sometimes Life Just "Happens".

Exercise:

Getting Support

What is happening in your life that causes you "not peace"?

Where can you get the support you need?

What simple concrete action can you take today that will support you in moving forward?

Journaling:

The End

Imagine what your life would be like if you had all the support you'd like and even more. Imagine knowing the Universe supports you, all the people around you support you and more! How would that show up? What would it look like and feel like?

The End

The number one most common regret at the end of life is: I wish I'd had the courage to live a life true to myself, not the life others expected of me.
~Bronnie Ware

Exercise:

In the End

Write your eulogy. What do you want people to say at your funeral? Hopefully it will be long into the future, but tap into it. What do you want to achieve, experience, create in this precious life you've been given? How do you want to be known? There are no right or wrong answers, only discoveries to be made in this exercise.

Journaling:

Life Unleashed

What is your dragon? What is the one thing that you absolutely don't want to turn around and face? It could be a conversation you need to have, really looking deeply at a financial drain or block or debt; It could be in your job, or family, or with friends. Look for it and find the dragon living in your mind. Dialog with it and discover why it's there and what you could do to become friends with it. Write in stream of consciousness form for 10 minutes or longer.

If-Only Drain

"Life should not be a journey to the grave with the intention of arriving safely in a pretty and well pre-served body, but rather to skid in broadside in a cloud of smoke, thoroughly used up, totally worn out, and loudly proclaiming "Wow! What a Ride!"
~ Hunter S. Thompson

Exercise:

If-Only Excuses

"If-Only-s." Here are a few to get your started. Mark the ones you identify with and list your own.

If only....
I was older
I was younger
I was married
I was single
I had kids
The kids were grown and on their own
I'd gone to school when I'd had the chance
I hadn't married/divorced/ him/her
I'd made a different choice a decade (or 5) ago
I was prettier
I was thinner
I was healthier
I was richer
I mattered
They understood me better
They... he... she... did or did not do what they did
I had better support

What else do you tell yourself?

These are your excuses. But what if they weren't there? What if you lived life full out – what would you do today? This year? This decade?

Journaling:

The Bucket List

What are your Bucket List items? List them here or if you don't have any, chose them now! Start with 10, then go with as many as you can imagine!

from Separation to Oneness

*We are always either contracting
or expanding.*

Exercise:

Stand Up and Claim Your Space

Stand up, if you can. Stand in the middle of your room and turn around. Look at what you see and notice what you notice. Feel a sense of contraction, feel the weight of the world on your shoulders, let your body collapse a bit and shrug down. Notice how that is for you. What do you think and feel in this place? When you are ready, stand up tall, throw your shoulders back, lengthen your spine and take a step across an invisible line into an expanded place. Notice how you feel now? Taller? Stronger? Freer? What else?

Make it a practice today to notice when you are contracted and consciously and physical expand. Stay in movement.

Take a few moments to write your realizations in this exercise.

Meditation:

Experiencing Oneness

Close your eyes and do some deep breathing. Feel your body sinking into the chair that you are sitting in. Become aware of the breath that you are breathing. Feel it entering and exiting your body with each inhale and exhale. Become aware of the air permeating and penetrating your entire being, both inside and outside. You are enveloped in the air, just like everyone else. Imagine a person across the globe breathing the same air that you are.

Feel your feet connecting to the ground below you. Draw your awareness down through your feet and into the ground, breathing up all that the earth has to support you. Feel your roots sinking deep into the planet, just like everyone else. Take a look at your body, each organ, muscle, bone. As separate and individual as they are, they compose You, your body, one organism.

As we are each individual and unique on the planet, all together, we comprise humanity, one species. We are not separate from each other or the planet. We are one, all together. Feel the expansive nature of this thought. We are one with the cosmos and the universe. We are connected by the breath we breathe, just as our bodies are connected by connected tissue. Become One with all that is. Become One with the earth and the sun. Feel the connection with a person across the globe. One heart, One humanity. Bask in this awareness of connection. We are One.

Take a few moments to write about this experience.

Get Your Gratitude On

The value of gratitude does not consist solely in getting you more blessings in the future. Without gratitude you cannot long keep from dissatisfied thought regarding things as they are.
~ Wallace Wattles

Exercise:

Get Your Gratitude Going

Make a gratitude list. List 30 things that you are grateful for. The first few will be easily apparent, but keep going, dig deep. What else are you grateful for?

Practice getting your gratitude on as often as you can remember it. Set a timer on your watch or cell phone for every hour. Each time activate gratitude consciously, from wherever you are.

Meditation:

Activating Gratitude

Let's activate gratitude now. Find a comfortable place to sit and set a timer for 10 minutes. Sit comfortably in your chair with your feet on the ground and your palms open. Take a few deep breaths in to center yourself. No matter what is going on in your life, become grateful. Yes, you can afford 10 minutes out of your busy day – it just might change everything.

Close your eyes and take a deep breath in. Feel the air entering your body. Feel gratitude for oxygen and the ability to breathe. Become aware of your body. How does it feel? Are there places of tension or tightness? Be grateful that you have a body, for the alternative is to not be alive at all. Become aware of the room you are sitting in. Be grateful for the roof over your head and the chair you are sitting on. Think about what you had to eat already today or a meal that is coming up. Be grateful that you have enough food to eat – much of the world does not. Think about your bed and how yummy it is to sink into the sheets beneath the covers at the end of the day. How grateful are you for the bed?

Put a smile on your face and feel the gratitude bubbling up from the center of your being, overflowing to the tips of your toes and fingers. Feel it rising up to the top of your head. Notice what is happening in your body. Do you feel differently? Still with your eyes closed, bring gratitude to your life situations. Even to the challenging ones and see what happens.

I'm so grateful. I'm so blessed.

Say these two statements to yourself a few times. Let them activate another level of gratitude. Say them out loud and claim them as true. I'm so grateful. I'm so blessed.

Anchor these statements into your being by placing your hands on your lower belly and saying them out loud three more times. Bask here for at least 10 minutes, or as long as you'd like.

When you are ready, say "I'm so grateful. I'm so blessed" one more time and gently open your eyes.

Take a few moments to write about your realizations and awareness.

Why We Are On the Planet:

Journaling:

Vocational Arousal

Sit quietly and listen to the impulse of vocational arousal within you. What are you being called to be or do? Is there something there that you haven't noticed before? Become the investigator of your Soul's desires. What is wanting to be birthed and expressed? Dig around and explore what is being revealed. What are the qualities underneath the impulse? And what else? Allow yourself time to write in a stream of consciousness manner, allowing the words and thoughts to be poured onto the paper, perhaps activating a new possibility and expression?

Exercise:

Investigating Your Life

If you believed you could do (what you listed above) what would you be doing?

Believing?

Seeing?

Tasting?

Hearing?

What new beliefs would you need to embody to be successful?

What else do you notice?

Self-Esteem: Coming to Love Yourself

*You can only love another to the degree
you love yourself. Love yourself more!*

Exercise:

The Truth About You

Where is your self-esteem on a scale of 1 – 10? 1 being in the tank, and 10 being totally confident and comfortable in your skin.

1   2   3   4   5   6   7   8   9   10

Are there places that you know you withhold from the world, to keep the peace, to not rock the boat, to maintain status quo? Are there ways that you feel fake? If so, list them here:

Make a list here of all the amazing, cool, uniquely you, things about you. What do you really like? Make this list at least as long as the previous one.

Meditation:

Choose Love

Sit comfortably in your chair and close your eyes. Take a few long slow deep breaths. Allow your body to begin to relax. Bring your awareness to your feet, feeling them connected to the ground and the earth below. Allow any tension to be drawn down through your feet and into the earth.

Let your shoulders relax and your breathing regulate. Imagine seeing yourself on a screen in front of you, this screen is your life. See yourself as you are today in the center of the screen. Let your eyes be soft with compassion and love. See a time line, with the past to the left and the future to the right. Move along the timeline until you find yourself as a very young baby. Let the image of your current self, pick that baby up and love her/him. Cuddle the baby, love the baby, snuggle it and talk to it about how incredibly wonderful, beautiful, smart, precious is it to you. Become the baby being loved on. How does that feel? Do you feel loved and cherished? Precious and adored?

Allow yourself to be loved so deeply that it surpasses all else. Begin to move along the time line from infant towards the present, bringing and integrating a deep self-love along the way, from toddler, to preschooler; from school age to teens, into your 20s, 30s, and all the way up to your current age. Feel the love, the compassion, the deep acceptance of the well-loved baby all the way through to current time.

Let the deep love permeate and penetrate your being, gently washing away anything unlike love. Bask in self-love, bask in acceptance and deep appreciation for the baby that you were and the adult that you are. Let a new state of being integrate through your consciousness. Right now, choose love. When you are ready, put your hands on your heart and say, "I love myself so very, very much!". Say it over and over until you believe it with every fiber of your being. Take a few deep breaths allowing the new consciousness to integrate fully.

Take a few minutes to write about your experience and how it feels to deeply love yourself.

Finding Ease in the Better

Some days "better" is the best it's going to be.

Journaling:

Better and Better

How could your life be better? How could life get just a little easier? What would that look like, specifically. Journal for 5 minutes about what better and easier would be.

Exercise:

Changing Perspective

Stand up if you are comfortable doing so, in the center of a room. Without turning your head, notice what you can see. Go into a corner of the room and facing the corner, notice what you can see from there. Not much, since you are looking right into a corner. Returning to the center of the room, look down at your feet. Again without turning your head, what can you see? Now look up. Notice how your periphery changes and that your vision becomes wider. Now go outside if you can and look up again. This time you can see more, especially if your view is wide open skies.

Look down again and think of your challenge, or discontent. See how limiting your thinking and vision becomes. Look up to the sky and see how possibilities arise. How can life get a little better? How can life get a little easier? Look up and allow an answer to appear in your being. It might be a quiet idea or a new question to ask.

Take a few moments to write about your insights in this exercise.

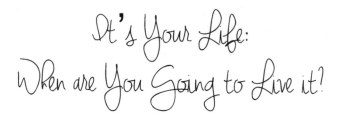

It's Your Life:
When are You Going to Live it?

"Our deepest fear is not that we are inadequate. Our deepest fear is that we are powerful beyond measure. It is our light, not our darkness that most frightens us. We ask ourselves, Who am I to be brilliant, gorgeous, talented, fabulous? Actually, who are you not to be? You are a child of God. Your playing small does not serve the world. There is nothing enlightened about shrinking so that other people won't feel insecure around you. We are all meant to shine, as children do. We were born to make manifest the glory of God that is within us. It's not just in some of us; it's in everyone. And as we let our own light shine, we unconsciously give other people permission to do the same. As we are liberated from our own fear, our presence automatically liberates others."
~ Marianne Williamson

Exercise:

Owning Your Brilliance

If you were powerful beyond measure, what would you think, say or do?

How would it feel? How would you be different?

Do you feel you have the right to be brilliant, gorgeous, talented, fabulous?

Is there a voice or feeling that resists owning that
right?

What if you stepped in to the Truth of who you are
here to be?

What if you recognized that most of your suffering comes from NOT being that and being distracted by life instead? Who might you be?

How could you come out in a new way and live a life of ease?

Meditation:

The Energy of Yes!

Sit comfortably and close your eyes. Take a few deep breaths in and out. Become aware of your feet on the ground. Open your palms and open your heart to receive. Drop into your heart space and rest there until your body, mind and spirit relax. From the depths of your heart, feel into the energy of Yes! How does that feel?

Notice the places that are screaming, "No!". Just notice and become curious once again.

Let the energy of Yes expand into a big circle of positive energy all around you. Let the Yes begin to embrace the No, gently bringing it from the outside to the inner circle. Can you claim a new life? Can you begin to imagine what life would be like if you claimed your brilliance? It's a game changer for sure! Play with the energy of Yes! for as long as you'd like. Give yourself questions and possibilities and let the Yes expand further.

If or when you notice a No creeping up, simply allow it and embrace it, bringing it along into the Yes. If the No is resistant, talk to it. It most likely is trying to keep you safe. Bring it into Yes again and again. When you are ready, bring the Yes into your body and anchor it by placing your hands on your lower abdomen and saying Yes, yes, yes. Take another deep breath in and exhale. Gently open your eyes.

Take a few moments to write about your experience with Yes!

Exercise:

If Life Sucks

If your life sucks right now – get help. Here are a few suggestions to get you going. List the ways that you will reach out to receive the help you need.

Talk to a counselor / therapist
Call a friend
Find a support group
Hire a spiritual coach (that could be me, ☺)
Read a book
Have a cup of tea
Find an attorney

List your actions here:

Closing Thoughts

How can life get easier?
Move from an energetic sense of contraction to
expansion. Shift from tight to open; from tense to
relaxed. It will work every time – guaranteed!
The simple thing to do and remember every time
is to move from an energetic sense of contracting
to expansion. Do whatever you can to shift from
tight to open, from tense to relaxed.

Exercise:

Unclench Your Being

Stand up and notice how your body feels. Contract it by scrunching up your shoulders, hunching over, tightening your fists and clenching your jaw. Notice what you notice. Now stand up, take a step away and expand. Open your posture, drop your shoulders and throw them back, open your fists, unclench your jaw and move a bit.

Notice where you might be tight in your body and stretch it open. Opening your body will open your mind and emotions. Stretch and expand.

Sit in a chair or lay down. Move through your body from the toes up to the top of your head, tensing and relaxing each area.

Begin with your toes and feet. Tense them up, hold for 10 seconds relax.

Calves and ankles – tense, hold and relax.

Knees and upper legs – tense, hold and relax.

Hips and butt
Belly
Diaphragm
Chest
Hands and arms
Back
Neck
Jaw and face
Scalp

Notice if there is any other tension in your body. If so, focus on it, tense it up and hold, then relax deeply. You are now deeply relaxed and tension free. Use the same technique on your emotions if they are running. Rest here, focusing on your breathing for as long as you'd like.

Journaling:

The Life You Love

You have begun to identify your hearts desires and the things you would love, released and cleared much of what has been in the way, now it is time to create and activate the life you love! Take a few minutes now to contemplate what you have learned and how you have grown through this guidebook. Where are you now compared to when you started reading the book and working the exercises in this guidebook. What are your big Ah-ha's and take aways? Then write a paragraph of your life like you would love it to be! Use your senses and write present tense.

About the Author

Touching hearts, freeing souls and transforming lives. Aliza Bloom Robinson, vibrational catalyst, speaker, author and minister is committed to the end of struggle and suffering on this planet. Having been an Ordained Unity Minister for over 16 years, Aliza has seen it all.

She has walked people through the depths of despair, agonizing heartbreaks, life changes and the heights of celebration. As a speaker and facilitator she commands the room with presence, humor and passion.

Aliza's first book, *Be a BOA, Not a Constrictor,* available as an eBook on Kindle, is an inspired fable for authentic transformation, becoming BOA; Bold, Outrageous, Authentic. She also is a contributing author in the Best Selling 365 Series, *365 Ways to Connect with Your Soul* and *365 Moments of Grace.*

And if you haven't downloaded the meditation that accompanies this book and "Falling Into Ease" you can get that here:

http://alizabloom.com/ease-meditation-freebie/

How to Work with Me:

Have you "fallen into Ease?"

I'd love to hear from you! What did you learn? What exercises were most impactful? Message me through Facebook or Email at:
aliza@alizabloom.com

If you have been inspired by the tips, tools, techniques and stories of this book and want personalized help to end your own suffering? Let's make that happen!

Join My Virtual Community by visiting me at:
http://www.AlizaBloom.com

Follow me on Twitter: @AlizaBloom

CPSIA information can be obtained
at www.ICGtesting.com
Printed in the USA
FFOW03n0543111217
43992834-43161FF